A Message Back
and Other Furors

A MESSAGE BACK

AND OTHER FURORS

Leonard Schwartz

CHAX 2008

Parts of this poem appeared, in slightly different form, in *Atlas, Golden
Handcuffs Review, Harper's,* and *Verse.*

Published by Chax Press in 2008

ISBN 978-0925904-79-9
Chax Press
650 East Ninth Street
Tucson, Arizona 85705-8584

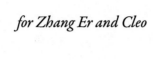

for Zhang Er and Cleo

contents

A Message Back
And Other Furors

//

Familiar ground is a foreign land.
Crates of cabbage, click of fruit bats,
every vertical surface either door
or daughter,
every horizontal a pots maw
or the juiciest, rawest,
most enchanting fruit ever drawn.
Beside one such clump of weeds I fall asleep
and the result is a poem,
either a cloud or a clown,
smart aleck. Either way
physical parting exacts crucial facts
amid panting breakers of foam.

//

The free signifier asks the unfree signifier
whatever,
and liberates its sense;
death palls.

//

Foreign to landscape (blah horizontal),
mindscape (pointless vertical), ur-scape (inauthentic),
but not to an elation produced by chant:
across a defamiliarized hill (neither nor)
scamper the strangest natural forms.
I would tell you what to look for
but mirrors are enemies of aura,
"you and "I' are both mirrors
and aura is everywhere, or so
I reflect, uttering "plaintive breakers"
 "defamiliarized hill", "strategic polytheism", etc.
Walla Walla somewhere out there,
whatever that means, while on the coast I boast
I'm at the edge of something's definition.
If imagination has its limit
how know as much without having
darted beyond it, eh smart aleck?
Mirrors are the enemy of all aura
other than their own.

//

Heaven brakes the falling fruit,
hoards it on the highest branch:
countless deaths below.

//

Uncanny under sense
that makes us sober and drunk.

The road follows behind
the first lines of morning.

If you recreate creation
questions come back as kids.

Door: towering daughter:
Cézanne's vatic cauldron.

Recreational vehicle
and the vehicle of recreation

Aligned on the easel
of ill-at-ease.

It isn't the plastic's fault
if it wakes up a cell phone.

//

How ask seven days to flower.
How ask seven days to flower as one creation.
How ask seven days to flower as one creation
in a single second of apperception.

//

Familiar ground is a foreign land.
Every vertical surface, either door.
Every horizontal a pots maw,
most enchanting fruit ever drawn.
And the result is a poem,
asshole. Either way.
Amid twittering breakers of foam.

Mindscape (rigorous, pointless),
goat gate (Provence),
defoliated hill (I didn't do it).
Purloined books tell me what to look for:
effluvia, everywhere,
plus "strategic polytheism".
While on the coast you badger
"you still droning on about the limit ,
you son of a fish?"
A) Most days seem a screen,
a play of divisions,
houses for this short comedy.
B) I think, therefore I have an office.

//

From the fen of the body politic
arise commands
that quicken the pace
of individual deaths,
dense with purposelessness.

//

Crates of cabbage, click of fruit bats,
or daughter,
or the juiciest, rawest.
Beside one such clod I fall asleep,
either a cloud or a clown.
Otherwise parting physically the crucial factor.
This office is only this office in winter.

Spring brings an elation produced by rant.
And the strangest natural forms.
Pssst: mirrors are enemies of aura.
Be refractory, my "wild breakers of foam".
Walla Walla somewhere out there,
at the limit of something's definition.

Swept from staggering vistas
to a tea pot in pieces.

Less than a whisper
with tickets reading Seattle, Los Angeles,
Tucson ... the bus performs eternity
and is the motion.

Mirrors/animas/particles of sand.

//

The deeper one delves into the surf,
the further the shore,
more profound the loss of memory.

//

Familiar land is a foreign ground.
Zero built its nest in These States.
Some people naked, others partly clothed.
How many gods people the thundering hall?
Words are animals that want to run away,
deer startled at the sight of mental agitation.
And being each and all unfurnished
when the grass and flowers are all gone
Americans awake in the artificial light of a large hall.
Our preference: not to observe that we are used like things.
Such obedience to cause and effect, action and sound.
Everything in this world is made to fit.
Everyone in the world works to make it fit.
It is fitting that everyone in the world should so work.
In winter I experience autumn's losses.
Spring fosters an awareness of that loss.
In summer, just summer, just this once.

//

Human remains remain human.

//

Familiar land is a foreign ground.
Some nudes escape, others partly clothe.
Animals the words that decide to run away forever.
Being each and all furnished with waves we don't need
we Americans awake in the morning to high tide.
Such obedience to cause and effect, action and sound.
Everyone in the world works to make it fit,
after all zero built is nest in these States.
How many natures people the thundering howl ?
Elk startled at the sight of mental agitation.
Grass and flowers, mostly gone.
Come on in, see how we are used like things.
Everything in this world is made to fit.
It is fitting that everyone in the world work.
Too ephemeral to merit further attention.
Too ephemeral these my tiny bones partition me.
Wild breakers from Howl rip apart the homes.

//

Misfortune's most holy site:
bleached by bomb light,
             mantel and bone.

//

Encased in shoes
feet clump down the staircases.
Car's doors close,
the sound of rush hour, sealing.
But between the word
and the social body,
utterance and act?
Not cause and effect
but convolution and defect,
caw and infect.
Tussle of language leading
some effort towards syntax
chaotic as its lore.
Cause and effect,
ash to be blessed.
Clause to be lauded,
a polyphony of geese.
Because. That is a fact.
Which is:
unfed panthers,
you son of an antler.
Star-69 that last
vowel-consonant cluster,
see what comes to
the proffered ear first.

//

Human remains remain human
makes for an emotional humus.

It is a peculiar step taken in painting
this great, realistic side,
the addition of a few fresh
ripe strawberries.

Its sleek, attractive look
will replace messy ice buckets.

//

Hidden from April to April
I have this confidence
in a special state
of unconscious immanence,
S-shaped emotion
like a huge kite whose string
somehow keeps unwinding...

//

So night rewards our mortality
with passion that shakes
the fictive order...
night, meaning Night,
drowns in a conglomerate
gestures of the hands
wherever an art appears
older than this tethered horse.

//

So there is a lifting.
It is in the listening.

Though swallowed by a whale
the first written document
remains a part of our oral life
every time we spout.

You are fighting how?
Yes, it's tempting for the voice
to locate correspondence in the hear
and noun,
but it has been a long time since
we've corresponded.

Yes, this culture gives me its claw
to claw it to pieces
but I'm so implicated in the culture
my least feint makes me afraid.
Self is presence to self,
self is presence to self.
A wreck tearing its own wreckage
thinks it sees a purpose in its acts,
figures that purpose makes it whole.

//

For which reason
a faux reign is established
in the desert provinces.
For rain will fall there finally,
whether we will it or no.
Soldier, amidst these disorders
flaunt your fairy god-mother.

//

Soldier, please don't forget the sea,
please turn from those
who slander the Atlantic,
the Pacific, the Arabic
oceans that are our Home :
analyze each slanderers motives,
flaunt your fairy godmother.
Each letter of each word
turns a roundabout;
pirates of all races really will be
turned to porpoises.
Every waking returns to sleep
but every sleeps return to waking?
The violent smack of a beavers tail
on water.
Peacocks wander
the unploughed paths of language.
I open my mouth: bonfires
blight a place of exile.
Cistern, spirit whirlwind,
rail track into a secret route
I refuse to clobber or saint.

//

Human remains remain human;
some humans apparently don't.

After months of exposure to the blistering sun
comes a lyrical protest against the dominion of prose.

Uncertainty
extends to the very roots of our slumber.

//

Millions went into the streets,
said "no" to the war, and meant it.

Not to abandon nothingness either,
that refusal to make up something
objective to mirror or wave:
that other, liberating form of "no"
only an individual can utter.

No contradiction? No contradiction.
No contradiction that will not make rich
a humus of resistance.

//

Human remains remain human
but not the particular humans they once held.

As people desperately scramble for cover
it is only to be expected that we will
mouth adjectives.

Most nights its steak, sweet potatoes,
and broccoli.

(How must one respond to this description
to say one grasps it?)

//

So there is a lifting. It is in the listening.

Deep night almost dams up all color, Selene's elation at being prime bearer of differentiation but for the indistinct murmurs of stars and that one red meteor.

No botany at all of course in a book without room for the forest we are all locked into and climbing. Unless I give things a little nudge and enter the clearing in animal form, pieces of plant twined in my fur. But I haven't yet decided on a mode of travel.

By morning moss seeks me out to be its bearded shadow.

Sign on the dotted soil if you want in on this thing. (The reeds are everything, I swear it.)

Contractually sacred.

In the beginning is the old life.

//

Human remains remain human;
human remains are all that remain.

Outside the inn
hordes of people.

For them the future
held no hope whatsoever.

Simply lived like everyone else,
without any inkling

of the madness
that was our common cot.

//

These myths enlist you
and the myth of you,
in a counter-myth
and a counter-myth of you
the ear is the off-shoot of,
between the flying geese
and the washed dishes,
moon and constellations.

Psst:

Never were we more free
than under the Germans.

So Sartre wrote of the Occupation.

Every action, every word,
a form of resistance,
a conscious choice.

Such that:
never are we less free
than as these occupiers.

//

Stop this war
with last night's
full moon.

How strive for the sun
when I cannot read my wife's mood?

And he struck right beneath the collar-bone
and the pointed bronze head tore clean through
and came out the base of his opponents shoulder.
 - The Iliad

So suffering is cured by suffering more,
according to Miguel Unamuno: a flock
of doves roped together.

Every waking returns to weep;
Miguel, release the rope.

//

Because we didn't speak yesterday they will bury us today.

They will whisper "for you to speak of coverlet, sheets, pillow and other bedding is simple nostalgia."

The bathers lie sprawled, far from warm baths.

We aren't anybody and yet are harnessed to the cart, a non-life that only works by clock-time.

And displaced waters in the occupied territories rise, as greater occupying weight is dropped. This run-off is spliced into some other media.

Perhaps the day when there will be no more _____ is not far off, the ethnic cleanser said to his wife.

The smiler is sleeping, all roads lead to his now narrow mouth.

Sorrow splits the homogeneity.

Some other kind of comfort, toward dawn, when folks are tired.

I can't wait for the day when all walls will finally be psychoanalyzed.

//

Human remains remain human.

A telescope's range in the palm of your hand.

Scavengers lurk and are deliberately kept abstract.

//

The word a mist amidst
glaciers and cliffs, aura bent into
imposing symmetrical progression.

More eager than plant or beast
the word does not condense its own emptiness
into a content twice in the history of words
or even once, one word simply
following another.

An orgy of texture permeating all things,
wander-lusted wilderness
capable of vocalization
only as the bewilderment.

Go with this venture, one word
right after another.

I just dropped my pancake on the ground,
it's all muddy.

Did you hear about the dictionary?
It turns out its just a book of quotations.

//

Quickened by all example,
autumn now begins to flow deeply
under the spell of fictions that do not fall,
fish still in the water.

//

One says something, then stops. The other says something else, perhaps stops.

A wasteful glance, observing nothing, foreseeing nothing, not even marking its own negativity, not even a glance, not even a waste... remember that night negotiating a plastic spoon? Not even that. Or maybe a face sketched on a napkin.

The eye reaches across this flowering medium, white as jasmine.

The sweet tumble of her garments exceeds the reality of the interacting garments themselves.

A Nothingness, a Nakedness, as of political refugees.

1) I gulped down the story.

Telling it to myself later triggered digestion.

2) When they pronounce my name I am really present.

But perhaps the other never really spoke.

//

Rime rules the mind in sneaky ways:
lore loves to joke.

//

A giggling fit shows literary brilliance.

I komodo dragon a passing cow.

A giggling fit is obliged to hire a secretary to answer its letters.

I monitor lizard the traffic cop speeding past my Bug.

A giggling fit tortured by the memory of a friend's death.

I basilisk the church, it becomes a basilica.

A giggling fit sentenced to some days of house arrest.

I anole everything that came before us.

A giggling fit inviting the snail to show its horns.

I bearded dragon the best minds of my generation,
discover the stillness at the heart of time.

The giggling fit: exonerated from all charges.

I uromastyx my steak with a vegetarians gusto for tofu.

A giggling fit in noncomplicity with homegrown aggression.

I iguana, you iguana, he, she, it iguanas.
We iguana, you iguana, they iguanatone.

A giggling fit a species has awaited for centuries.

I chameleon Charlemagne onto our team,
then Richard the Lion-Hearted.
Everybody, into the blender!

The giggling fit: inferior in business acumen.

I Tokay gecko my way up the mirror, never once noticing
the mirror is not OK with this intrusion.

A giggling fit confounds all opposites and spins a sphere.

I newt the difference, we slip back and forth
between both coasts, we believe in our own basic wetness.

A giggling fit exchanging pillows with a giggling fit.

I caiman one door and went out the other
aquifer: you caiman the same door
but got caught by the Romans.

A giggling fit with seven strings.

I spiny lizard so ardently you must spin
zillions of yarns to fend me off.

A giggling fit when the match is struck.

I Cuban anole the cracks in my cabin.
Ten minutes later I'm suffocating.

A giggling fit diagnosed as pregnant with quintuplets
instead gives birth to an encyclopedia of forms.

I lizard each one of The Ten Commandments.

//

(I am going to convert my face into a condominium,
then turn my face to the East.)

(I'm planning out my future face along a cautious investment strategy
since I've already messengered over to you the imprint of my fists

And it would be imprudent of me not to expect
a message back, your ammo belt around my neck

And other furors.)

(I am going to advocate for a shorter attention span
across class lines, as a way of creating a greater commonweal.)

(I plan to invest in a line of houseboats
without any floors – driftwood really.)

(I'm going to install a program that enables for shorter attention spans
under the auspices of helping people forget they have slaves.)

(I am going to replace phenomenology with foamenology,
foamenology with firmenology, I am committed to something firm.)

//

Imagine that a period is ending in your life.
Then a comma. Then a line break.

The flower absent from all bouquets
shines in grottoes and in your grammar,

More alluring than the obvious garden,
more obvious than manicured allure.

Tears the color of your eyes
ply your high cheekbones.

Have to stay on the edge of things
or both time and emotion will go flat.

And great piles of scallions piled in ice,
having just arrived from wherever they grew.

An inner sound, imagination noise,
rhythms inside an impassive slip of pearl-gray river.

Composing antithetical couplets,
the last god crouching in the crack between.

//

Then the rain came, beating the good
with the better, pooling in the wheel barrow

And the flower absent from all bouquets
tender with cold rain.

Flower that is never
a flower, flower that refuses

To be a flower:
namelessness/haunts/ punctuation.

Your attention please:
train #117, The Signifier,

Bound for Shapely Union,
making stops in Logos, Lyre,

Limpid, and Translator-Of-Desire,
is now boarding.

All ticketed passengers are invited to assemble
at the gate marked "Broken Mirror".

//

Woven into my melancholy a queen announced the arrival of spring.

Her appearance wrought a wreath in me, a secret rapport with some routine of the sunshine, a drop of milk where I'm only ropes.

Ceremonies of deep listening.

Doors startled open at the sound of mental things.

Apparently this is your present experience too since you have been writing again of a feather, telling again of our city and our oars, the story of our follies poised upright as candles, wicks dreaming, wax sworn to commemorate these certain holy days, and the books all functioning in a normative way.

According to observers myths are autonomous signifying systems.

Nine hags seated themselves in a semi-circle around my cot. Or else watchfulness impenetrably woven pours from the decanter into Elijah's cup.

Fjords rent the prose, the ear in you pilots you behind yourself.

The most important identification is the identification with the slaves.

Choir of the nearly inaudible.

//

You be the General.
Command Decisions.
What Is Your First Bombing Target?
A) Troops
B) Fuel Supplies
C) Roads
Friday 9:30 PM/8:30 C
The History Channel.
Click here to get into the action –

Picture of a man sitting on a sofa equipped with tank-treads. His feet are up, wearing sneakers, jeans, military vest and helmet. Presumably on the basis of this he is

into the action.

Well, OK then:

who should be our first bombing target?

//

House of the dead,
photographed world,
choir of the nearly inaudible.

Pilgrims to it
misname what they see
calling it "album"

And I am one of them,
misprision of myself and others
in hope of obtaining an end to the killing
I'm hopelessly a part of.

The silent ones, no longer real and not yet empty,
piled on the backs of diminutive donkeys.

High emotion always means... big trouble.
And the musical patterns are so near at hand.

//

I often see stars early in the morning.
They order me to surrender my keys and luggage.

If our plane takes off at 8 in the morning
will our souls still be able to escape our bodies at 8:26?

Some blossoms in the water do not reach the surface
of the water but grow entirely under water.
The role of the root to know itself slenderly.

In the absence of a root an even more slender knowledge.

You want to have your Odysseus
And Ulysses it too.

I am both of your directions.

//

Roar and rupture turn another page.
Black foam of syllabic count
overflows my cup.
From alpha soil you have come,
to alpha soil you will return,
so when do we get to "bet"?
The sea auditions its final wave,
wind on the way, rain and thunder too,
the soldier forgetful.
I voyage towards a moon
unchanged by syllogisms,
muteness romping like a minotaur
across the page, prevented
from running amuck
only by the page's maze.
And that other monster,
the monotaur Yahweh?
Pronoun unpronounceable.
A new pronoun grown old.
A nude pronoun: a provocation.
In any event, an old pro.

//

Everything to which we relate ourselves must itself turn away,
a carousel ride for which ticket you pay a bit of heart.

//

Your attention please:
train #71063, The Line of Spiders,
making stops in Smile As Fast As You Can,
Disconnects, The Book of Life, Glacial Glacial,
New Mouth, North Mouth, and Unfed Panther,
is now boarding.
All ticketed passengers are invited to proceed immediately
to the gate marked Star 69.
Those passengers holding tickets embellished
by previously unheard of vowel and consonant clusters
are invited to board the special Soft Sleeper
which will be located at the end of the Line of Spiders platform.
Amnot-Traceable would like to take this opportunity
to thank you for riding with us, and to remind you
it is impossible to make peace with the New Inquisition.
Your attention please:
train #71063, The Line of Spiders,
making stops in Smile As Fast As You Can,
Disconnects, The Book of Life, Glacial Glacial,
New Mouth, North Mouth, and Unfed Panther,
is now boarding. All ticketed passengers are invited
to proceed immediately to the gate marked Star 69.
Thank you.

//

That which is dependent upon breaks, lapses, non-communication, words skulking forth only at irregular intervals so that any one of them may later become intelligible, no name yet known for any one thing, no real things yet gumming up the works.

So mountains arise because of the absence of mountains and the absence of mountains arises because of mountains, and on and on, in a long chain.

So that nothing remains but this fragile tent of language filled with holes and pitched on the peak, this tent folded up each morning as if its answer to all darkness was the implausibility of awakening.

And yet this awakening, as if forgetting all pain within the articulated grace of it's own radiant necessity.

Not in the deep Night of Reason but in the simple night of anonymity will a wing start to flap.

Sensibility is an experimental procedure.

//

The five doors to the Temple are Desire, Surliness, Meditation, The Kiss, and Doodling.

The four corridors that lead from these doors are Derealization, Dissonance, Sleepy Hollow, and The Light of the Face.

Who amongst us wouldn't want to write the sequel to *The Magic Flute*?

After that, the tabernacle.

In the tabernacle, the two tablets.

What is written on one of the two tablets behind the screen opposes what is written on the other tablet behind the screen. At every point.

The first tablet says the world is a word. The second tablet has a hole punched through the middle and leads outside.

See, I told you, a vast mountain chain.

//

In a recently refurbished auditorium, individualized right down to its tiniest follicle, a wing starts to flap, making a specific sound. How many peoples populate these thundering halls? Millions went into the streets, said "no" to the war, and meant it.

I have always preferred these streets to the tabernacle. Even after I made my first visit to The Architecture Underworld, and saw all those ghosts of buildings, and the tabernacle too, grieving.

The street through Architecture Underworld was recognizably of our world. It seems streets don't die, they just keep on going, a kind of sprawl. Yet The Library of Alexandria, The Twin Towers, and The First Temple, lined its quotidian.

My recently refurbished auditorium stood on the intersection of that street too, its address obscured, in all its uncanny specificity.

The sacred and the profane are sacred.

//

The chair that stands at the end of a certain kind of carpenter-
ing differs from the mountains that have clambered so high for
simple recreation.

Said chair was made for a purpose, at a price.

Said chair will never grow.

The idea of new light sounds from beneath the visible edifice but
head phoned soldiers receive another, more aggressive message
from their bosses.

O Cultic consciousness capable of maintaining a community!

If threatened by a gap, break, pause or its own false step, said
consciousness will next ask of you sexual favors, in some unlikely
alcove simultaneously aesthetic and political, the facts of logi-
cal space dissolving along with any sense of confidence in your
power, or its.

//

In our country said cultic consciousness is mighty strong – but not unquestioned.

Aiming to retrieve the authority of the original myth, and thus to restore its own efficacy, said cultic consciousness lusts yet again to possess your mind and flesh.

Instead it finds itself grasping a sack of old bones – its own destiny!

While the "beloved" – the free individual, you and me - beholds a billy goat pushing its way through a crowd of people, or a chair bolted to the earth, in which this individual – any of us - is told to sit for questioning.

That chair will never grow, unlike the list of those told to sit.

//

From their first articulation in colloquial French in 1927 sexual relationships wrought confusion. The earth filled with violence attributable to sexual love: actually the very word " love" originally referred to a form of half serious, half playful spanking.

Happiness courts the light, and so my identity begins. From my birth seem to issue threads from all those innumerable worlds of the gods, the lichen and the bark.

A path opens up in front of even someone who knows nothing, living and dying in this single exchange, just as the radiant light of the gods slaps the bourgeoisie like a fish already flung on deck, beating against the planks.

The original scheme of the garden lends itself to the new one.

What an unusual admixture at the bottom of silence!

Quickened by all example, autumn now begins to flow deeply under the spell of fictions that do not fall, fish still in the water.

//

All passengers ticketed *for Speculum Flight #4434, bound for Manhattan Mausoleum Municipal Airport: that flight has already departed. The next scheduled Speculum Flight to MMM, flight #8116, is scheduled to leave in four minutes. Passengers from the late arriving Speculum Flight #5, originating in Syntax, those of you who were ticketed for flight #4434 to Manhattan Mausoleum, would do well to approach the Speculum ticket agent and ask for permission to board Flight #8116.*

Speculum Airlines would like to announce that Flight #4434, bound for MMM, has already departed No Root International Airport. Passengers from late arriving Speculum Flight #5, Originating in Syntax and changing here in MMM, are advised to plead with the ticket agent for a place on Flight #8116, also bound for Manhattan Mausoleum. This will be the last flight from No Root to Manhattan Mausoleum this evening. There will not be enough seats for everyone. Thank you for your patience.

//

If we are able to believe in contradictory things
it is because those battles have passed into the language as truce.
If we are unable to believe in contradictory things the war rages on.
If we are able to believe in contradictory things
this means we can compartmentalize our bodies and our brains.
If we are unable to believe in contradictory things
this means we have achieved a unity of body and mind.
The warrior achieves a unity of body/mind by purposeful action.
The State of The Union is strong.
The State of Contradiction is strong.
The State of Non-Contradiction is strong.

If we are able to believe in contradictory things
it is because violence is accepted as a legitimate political instrument.
If we are unable to believe in contradictory things
this means we will not see what will come to pass without us.
If we are able to believe in contradictory things
it means that the hives are filled with gun powder.
If we are unable to believe in contradictory things
it means the gun powder is filled with the nastiest bees.
The warrior achieves a unity of hive and powder.
The State of the Union is strong.
The State of Contradiction is strong.
The State of Non-Contradiction is strong.

If we are able to believe in contradictory things
The butter moon follows strict protocols of disclosure.
If we are unable to believe in contradictory things
the mitten-shaped leaves barely bother to wave.
If we are able to believe in contradictory things
all speakers need to shut up or step up or neither or both.
If we are unable to believe in contradictory things
a voice that decompresses a persons parts does the talking.
The State of the Union, the State of Contradiction
and the State of Non-Contradiction are all strong.

If we are able to believe in contradictory things that means
one hour in heaven, one in hell, and the rest of time in purgatory.
If we are unable to believe in contradictory things
the journey of interiority means a trip to the liquor store.
If we are able to believe in contradictory things I feel that
I am one of them, and share in the silence of being.
If we are unable to believe in contradictory things
I am flightless, an authentic grave, and never other.
The State of the Union is grave.
The State of Contradiction is grave.
The State of Non-Contradiction is grave.
In any case, recurrence is a definite no-no.

//

Clear thought stops short
workers up at dawn.

Bus ride along a waterfront lined
by the most deplorable infirmities,

The great melancholy tide of
my coming to you at all costs.

The blind wall fails to realize its bind:
its blind, and its bound, and things only bump or hang from it.

Green moons of sorrow go to the movies.
I am filmed burying a cow.

During the previews I buy three ice cubes.
They are contorted and full of wrinkles and plainly not ice.

Of course only a fraction of what is felt
survives as redemptive

While violence obliterates everyone who humors
its missionaries, those puppets of appropriation.

Thus I offer cocoa to the ferns, first form of the downtrodden.
Just outside the frame I am birthing a cow - no really.

Chance so rarely conflicts with intelligence,
that I announce: "enough with the proverbs."

68

A moment of fright as some shriveled embers
integrate with a comprehensive view of evil.

//

Infinity spreads across a single face,
smile in an instant lost behind contingent armor.

Only this chiasm reveals infinity,
tiny flood of bewilderment atwinkle in the flesh.

How I love it that your love has seen you through,
that the shadows that rustle in your vocabulary are true

We who can only dream of a language whose words
are steeped in the language of sacred dance.

For virtually all other expression is a subterfuge intellect attempts
passionately to penetrate, or barks at like a puzzled dog.

For virtually all expression is subterfuge, save the spread
of the infinite joke, our patience in waiting for the punch line.

Or even though half one's face is literally gone,
a lute lifts in the beloved's blood

Much of subjectivity figuratively discredited
yet a contemporary logos within the lute

Still lit late, still limned late,
figured in the lyric, heard in the head

Looks up at the moon and feels
the hairs on their body stand on end

Wanders the Lower East Side
like a ghost, pleading to be permitted to finish her poem

Thumbs through Kentucky phone books
looking for runes amongst the crowd of clustered names.

Ours is said to be a world gone dabchick,
drawing down a veiled curtain over the Owl.

Yet after the poem is chopped up into thousands of bits
it is reborn as itself, somehow the same.

The words need not disseminate broadly
and will not disseminate broadly, in order to be words.

Poet, be the odd man out, obviously,
a season in the sea's romance with land.

As the translator of desire wrote in his notebook:
"the signifier and the signified were deer in the headlights".

//

The goddess Isis intervenes amongst animals grazing
in the meadow: a donkey is about that isn't
ordinary, and he is in love with a woman.

Wordsworth's "real, solid, world of images":
feathered serpents appear frequently in my sleep,
batting against the flimsy screen, wanting me.

The girl turned into a frog.
The frog wore the weary look
of fatherhood.

They sacrificed the dog; he came back to life.
Then that dog was happy, and wagged his tail.
All our dogs wag their tails too.

The sun bittern resembles
the sun-flecked forest interior,
source of my joy revealed when she takes wing.

The other source is communicative humor
trumped by triumphal metamorphosis
seven butterflies in a row.

Converging rivers and the "I" of which
I am conscious are both part of my heritage,
and together they remove the harness from the horse.

To go and eat in a restaurant
is truly a strange experience,
like reading a book.

Bewilderment
Is the only ark.

CODA (RED FOG)

A red fog occupied both the cities and the hinterlands.

After the collective memory of a time before the fog begins to
miniaturize itself, turning into a key that slips from a parents
pocket while playing with his child in the grass; after the wild
grasping hands of beings unlike ourselves withdraw into the
wood; after the absolute alarm of flesh succumbs to the infirmity
of the mind in its failure to imagine flesh alight; after the alabas-
ter alarm clock of the self began to ring and ring and ring - deep
in what sleep, deep in what sleep? - or after the words have bed-
ded down for the night; after the night unfurls over the empty
headlands and the wind offers ultimatums to the exhausted sand:
after the laughter of the ocean shakes the fulcrum of my being;
after the rain cloud exhausts every drop of its discharge and exists
only as kneeling puddles and slinking eddies sinking ever lower
on the plain; then, a spiral motion.

You believe in perceptions, in forms, in bodies, in perceptions
of forms and bodies, but these are all maps, the perceptions, the
bodies, the forms. You choose to look at them – the bodies and
the forms – but there are no maps onto which to place what you
see, no charts with which to freeze what you feel, no maps or
charts to deploy in order to traverse or conquer this field. The
word "map", like the word "God", a vile obscenity. This obscen-
ity fills my work with spiral voids. A cat chases a red point of
light shot from a pointer, a moving beam impossible to paw,
impossible for pussy not to pursue: red beam projects red point,
red beam traceable back to held pointer, a watch in the sand by

the shore. Words are beamed without point. Thus she chose to remain wordless, would not utter a single sound. She spoke. Thus, a spiral motion.

After the city had been abandoned and the dog had begun to bark, after the conversation with difference ended, the limp that came in and the imp that went out; after the gaps between "A" and "B" and between "C" and "D" failed to reveal any unsuspected images and sounds; after self-contemplation was reconfigured as elf immolation, the well-spring of pent-up waters left so pent, or allowed to rush as inexact vocabulary into an immovable glacier, tense with the effort that drives off what I intended to maintain by effort, relaxing and letting drop what I intended to preserve, doubting in the words I helped elicit in the other, the one I was speaking to and helping to speak and investing my own energy in the speech of. In other words: am I a man dreaming I'm a spiral motion, or a spiral motion dreaming I'm in dialogue? The heart-held camera only shows us what it wants to show us in any given beat.

After the rabbit had been eaten and the cigar burned so low it refused to be relit; after switching one word with another word and watching them both burn up in their new locations; after the mind failed to fill in the space around it with an aesthetic of its own compulsion; after the words had become weighted with their worst associations, yet still were recognizable as what

they had been before and thus did not become new words; after
the furrows in the field were covered with frost; after the frost
was speckled with some dark spore released by the action of the
frost working upon the field; after a mouse, trembling, exited
from his hole into the clear blue day: I spoke again into the
whirling void.

After the individual person had become a joke, after jokes be-
came the innermost substance of persons, after the rain fell and
dispersed the frost in cold eddies of water casting up mud and
drowning the spores; after a wind rose up again and froze the
outer scum of the pond and the rain that had fallen; after the
electricity poles where the birds used to perch suddenly stood
empty of both birds and wires; after a motorbike disturbed the
dusk; after a knife pasted to a board of wood, covered with paint,
suddenly flashed from inside the art work: the mind flashes, open
to its own ground: the spiral motion empties itself again of all
content -; after the stage collapses in the hilarity of its invention;
after the geese fly shrieking through the barely intelligible sky
and a potted plant is tipped over and dumps its soil on the always
soggy carpet, one or two half-broken clods crumbling through
a break in the screen, releasing one single crumb through the
screen, into the outside world: the dead electricity poles fill with
crows, the crows caw: she speaks into the spiral motion.

I spoke into the whirling void. After the privilege of the infinite turned out to be finite; after the mission of reading is felled by televised idols; when an extra step away from the desert road means to lose the road forever; after negation is called into question by a viscous goo of image that accumulates on everything, even on nothingness, especially on nothingness, until nothingness is goo; after the geese flew through a departing patch of orange sunlight: the glimmer of nothingness catches your eye from inside the spiral: it is possible to move again, into a new space, because of the split: the woods echo and crash in the throes of the tremor: the plates and glasses, the silverware, slide from the table -; after their crash, a great silence; after the great silence, a potential leaf pile; after the leaf-pile has been assembled and played in, its every audible crinkle savored and memorized and productive of new language in the aftermath, one that does not contain in it a word for "death" with the slightest negative connotation; then comes a spiral motion.

After amazed solitude solved its maze and became lonely, after golden eggs hatched into golden eaglets, after the sumptuous cradle grew too tiny to contain even the smallest of offspring, something smooth and pristine abandoning its own idea of itself for someone else's idea of it and becoming lumpy; after the dazzle of being and the razzle-dazzle of non-being; after a wax cast was slipped over a feverish living form, after the form in its fever melted all the wax and emerged from the drippings, even more

feverish than before, glistening, distorted, human; when the
guard barked at the visitor, mistaking him for a prisoner, and the
visitor drew further into the cluster of inmates, until the guard,
who would remain in the prison on a longer bid than the visitor
or any of the inmates, realized his mistake and utterly altered
his tone of voice, the voice suddenly the kind one human offers
to another, the willed change of which was more horrific in its
implications than the original snarl; after the ping-pong table,
set outdoors, warps beyond the hope of predictable bounce and
abandons all hope of garnering attention, beading with moss the
color of its own paint, its aluminum legs buckling in submission
to its pariah status; after the spongy terrain of syntax and forest
floor becomes its own raison d'etre, dotted with barely percep-
tible trails along which the postman must walk if he wants to
deliver the unretractable message; when the obscene word, shorn
of any other way of being uttered except as an obscenity, or of
being sent, except as an obscenity, sickens, gets ready to be said
but then grows silent: for words on their own can never weep:
the web is filled with living flies: long-forgotten wrecks tremble
in their undersea graves, as if suddenly, in spite of all, they had
expectations: the fish, swimming in spiraling schools around the
ruined hulk, are agitated too, as if anticipating a sudden change:
no wind, but all the pines along the shore-line bend slightly
towards the bay: the reader tosses aside his book and walks away
before anything happens, because nothing ever seems to really
happen: the captain jettisons half-filled barrels in anticipation of

a storm: the wanderer jettisons his rucksack and decides to stay
put, where he has come. Of these three only the wanderer finds
he must recant. He picks up his rucksack, spirals away.

There is no map. It is either a beach or a desert the wanderer
traverses, or both at once. After the plovers nest has been raided
and the plovers eggs have been eaten, after the walking dunes
have buried the wanderers footprints and the tiny broken egg
shells; after the wanderer has gone many miles along this strip
of land either coastal or arid or perhaps both at once; after
his wandering has become increasingly aimless and desper-
ate: - every living being desires to wander and change, but this
particular wanderer is already dead, having lost his argument
with his lungs, recanted everything his heart has pumped, or
so he feels as he wanders: - the ice-cube machine avalanches its
creations into the bucket, the bucket is carried excitedly along
the corridor back to the motel room, the cubes are dumped right
away into the sink: - immediately upon coming to rest in the
sink the ice begins to imperceptibly shift, those with ears discern
a slight trickle of movement as beads of water begin to melt, to
escape: - so the wanderer resting on his back in the soft sand feels
his being indiscernibly trickle into the beach, or was it a desert,
a ditch in the epistemic ground, grain upon grain of unique
matter stamped to the outline of his body; after he had slept in
that position for what seemed to him like an eternity; after he
had wondered how such a sleep was possible, to descend to such

depths and to be able to emerge from such depths, until he realized he was awake; after a brown regulation football was swept in by the waves and he realized that yes, here was the ocean, therefore this was definitely a beach, only possibly a desert; after the placebo of words had worn off, which is to say nothing had worn off because placebos never wear off, never having had an effect; after gathering himself up to watch the sun rise as if by some supreme effort of the will on the part of both the wanderer and the sun; after adjusting his black eye patch and tugging on his floppy black cap:- the sun rises over the sea:- men clamor for meaning, women clamor for freedom, children clamor for chump change:- in the gathering light, one of each lay in the hammock and shared a drink, passing the glass back and forth amongst themselves with some care: look, here come cows and horses being herded down the beach, or a spiral motion of sealed instructions, or a domestic camel mistaken for a wild camel: as if it was you was who was writing into this spiral void, the camel really wild and this a desert after all.

a note on the author

Leonard Schwartz is the author of numerous books of poetry and essays including, most recently, *Ear and Ethos* (Talisman House, 2005), *Language As Responsibility* (Tinfish 2007), and *The Tower Of Diverse Shores* (Talisman House 2002).

OTHer BOOKS From CHaX Press

2008 books from Chax Press include

Busy Dying, by Hilton Obenzinger (fiction)
Transducer, by Jeanne Heuving (poetry)
Sound Remains, by John Tritica (poetry)
Slightly Left of Thinking, by Steve McCaffery (poems, texts, and post-cognitions)
Implexures (complete edition), by Karen Mac Cormack (prose)
Environmental Reporter, by Dennis Williams (artist's book)
Wardolly, by Elizabeth Treadwell (poetry)
In Felt Treeling, by Michael Cross (poetry)
The Frank Poems, by C.A. Conrad (poetry)
and several others to be announced at a later time

Other recent books include

Jam Alerts, by Linh Dinh (poetry)
Since I Moved In, by Tim Peterson (poetry)
Swoon Noir, by Bruce Andrews (poetry)
Afterimage, by Charles Borkhuis (poetry)
Accidental Species, by Kass Fleisher (fiction)
Waterwork, by Sarah Riggs (poetry)
Mirth, by Linda Russo (poetry)
Witness, by Kathleen Fraser and Nancy Tokar Miller (handmade fine book edition)

Chax Press programs and publications are supported by donations from individuals and foundations, as well as from the Tucson Pima Arts Council and the Arizona Commission on the Arts, with funding from the State of Arizona and the National Endowment for the Arts.

Arizona
Commission
on the Arts

TUCSON PIMA
ARTS
COUNCIL

NATIONAL
ENDOWMENT
FOR THE ARTS